Los Cabos

A history of development, people, places, sea, and sun

Cover photo credit: Dr. Mark Schrader, El Arco, 2007, JPEG file.

Los Cabos

A history of development, people, places, sea, and sun

Dr. Mark Schrader

Editor: Kimberly Schrader

April 2020

Copyright © 2020 Dr. Mark Schrader

All rights reserved. This book or any portion thereof may not be reproduced or used in any manner whatsoever without the express written permission of the publisher except for the use of brief quotations in a book review or scholarly journal.

First Printing: 2020

ISBN: 978-0-578-23304-8

Publisher: Dr. Mark Schrader

https://autumnlanes.wixsite.com/loscabos.com

Dedication

To my lovely wife, Kim, and our family.

Thank you. Without your support and patience, I would have never achieved this project.

Contents

Quote..i
Forward...ii
The Book..1
The Author...36
Appendix..37

"Live in the sunshine, swim in the sea, it's time for something almost free"
— Cabo Beach Vendor

Foreword

The word "Cabo" used to bring visions of a small remote village known for its unparalleled sport fishing, beautiful beaches along the Sea of Cortez, the famous arch "El Arco," and a smattering of high-end resorts designed as playgrounds for the rich and famous. But when the area opened up to the crowds, it exploded in a boom of development. In the late 1950s, 10,000 acres of coastline could be bought for $15,000, and now eleven oceanfront residential properties in luxury developments sell for an average price of $12.6 million. Today, sprinkled across the coastline are the construction cranes that work feverishly to build the next sensational master-planned development, each advertising the highest possible trend in luxury destinations, complete with the ultimate in spa decadence, cuisine prepared by world-renowned chefs, extensive wine bars, infinity multi-tiered pools, and golf-laden bliss. How did this happen and in such a short time frame? This book is a collection of information on Cabo's past through to today's mega developments, a glimpse of those who played pivotal roles in its progress and a look at the area from then until now. Enjoy the journey of Cabo as I personally have for the past thirty-eight years!

It was 1988, and I had just completed the first Halloween Bash triathlon in Los Cabos, which ended in the small town of San Jose del Cabo. The run was along the single twenty-nine-mile two-lane highway that connects San Jose to Cabo San Lucas, and along the way one would have passed only four hotels on the coastline. Much has transpired over the years that has transformed this relatively unknown remote fishing village into one of the most desirable luxury resort locations in the world today. But how did this all happen? Along the way, I have gathered and read bits and pieces that have provided some insight, including that of various Cabo "pioneers," but have never really found a comprehensive answer.

In the early 1950s, the population was under three-hundred in Cabo San Lucas and no hotels existed there. In fact, there was not much there at all. In the photo below the mountain in the background and to the left is the Pedregal, center is the old Catholic church that exists today on Cabo San Lucas Street, and to the right of it is a house that is now MiCasa restaurant. Indeed, an amazing transformation from then to now.

(Photo: Cabo San Lucas, 1952. Photo given to Carol S. Billups.)

In 1950, the Hotel California, which was founded in 1947 by a Chinese immigrant named Mr. Wong, opened in Todos Santos when the population of the entire Baja Sur was just over 60,000. The only real business in Cabo at that time and the major employer of its three-hundred inhabitants was the old tuna cannery, which was initially established back in 1927. At its peak, it used to produce approximately 75% of Mexico's output of canned seafood products. The cannery first started out as a four-mast sailing ship anchored near the now famous arch. The ship burned and sank to the sea bottom however. Hence, the cannery building was built, and it was named Pando after the original owners. The shell of the building remains today, although the famous dock is no longer there as a result of Hurricane Juliette in 2001. It's to the right as you pass the mouth of today's Cabo San Lucas Harbor entrance on your way out to sea.

(Photo: Cabo San Lucas Cannery, Photo from an unknown source, found at the following site: bdoutdoors.com)

Word of the great sport fishing in the waters near and around Cabo was slowly getting out from the then rich and famous yacht owners who came to try their anglers' luck. It's hard to imagine the sheer amount of fish that existed then. Marlin and sailfish could be seen schooled en masse floating in the waters off Cabo, as evidenced in the 1949 short "Pacific Coast of Mexico." Access to this video clip can be found on youtube.com/watch?v=z9FNFXXucbo. As word spread, others took notice, including William Matt "Bud" Parr and Abelardo Luis "Rod" Rodriguez, the son of the former Mexican president. Both men are considered two of the original "pioneers" of Los Cabos today.

The governor of Baja California Sur, Agustin Olachea, a friend of the Rodriquez family, asked Rod Rodriguez to assist him in promoting an agricultural enterprise at Los Planes near La Paz. He was looking for help in building an airstrip there to transport produce to the Los Angeles market. In exchange for his help, Rod would be offered ownership in the project and a land deal at a discount. He was an avid aviator and flew his personal P51 down to La Paz to discuss the project, where he was offered by a local rancher named Juan Vivez an interest in selling a property named Rancho Las Cruces, a 10,000-acre ranch with five miles of coastline along the Sea of Cortez. The property is located just east of La Paz and just slightly southeast of Las Cruces on the coast. The agreed price was $15,000, and with that, the vison of Rod Rodriquez in developing the southern end of Baja would begin. He believed that a resort away from it all would be welcome relief to those who wanted to enjoy the serenity as well as a base for the excellent sportfishing. As a

Photo credit: Google Earth. See the guitar-shaped pool in lower left of photo which was built for Desi Arnaz.

result, in October of 1950, the Rancho Las Cruces Resort opened its doors with nine guestrooms, and a main building, supporting a 3,000 ft. airstrip. The success of the resort surpassed everyone's expectations, and by 1953 it was clear that the resort needed to expand. At that time, William "Bud" Parr, an avid sportsman and Southern California real estate investor, purchased a 50% stake in the resort giving it the capital to expand. By 1955, the resort was listed as one of the top ten luxury resorts, ranking second in the world, and attracted guests such as Tyrone Power, Clark Gable, Henry Fonda, Burt Lancaster, John Wayne, Bing Crosby, Dwight Eisenhower (he was fond of tending the BBQ for the quests), and Desi Arnaz, who built a house on the property, complete with a guitar-shaped pool. Later, when Matt Parr decided to move on to other developments, he sold his share to Bing Crosby, who built a home there as well. Today the hotel is also distinguishable by the three crosses perched on a point near the hotel overlooking the Sea of Cortez.

Photo credit with permission: Rancho Las Cruces.

Rancho Las Cruces was one of the first major luxury resorts in the Baja tip, with nothing yet planned in Cabo San Lucas or San Jose. Others existed, but on a different scale and further from the Los Cabos corridor, for example, the Flying Sportsman, built by Ed Tabor in Loretto in 1952, and Rancho Buena Vista, developed by Herb Tansey on the East Cape in 1952. Bud Parr clearly saw the potential of the area and in addition to the Las Cruces investment, he and Rod Rodriquez bought four-hundred acres in 1953 with a mile

Hotel Las Cruces Palmilla, 1956. Photo from an unknown source, found at the following site: gingogazette.com. Notice the 4,500 ft. long airstrip in photo at upper right.

of beachfront on the Sea of Cortez coastline just south of San Jose for $15,000. They jointly developed the property and, in 1956, with only fifteen rooms, opened the Hotel Las Cruces Palmilla, which is now known as the One & Only Palmilla. The resort set a new standard for luxury, and with Rod's wife, Lucille, who was a Hollywood actress, the celebrities flocked to this site via small planes, using the resorts 4,500-ft. airstrip. It became their perfect hideaway. In 1984 the resort was expanded to fifty-three suites, and in 1986 the Koll Company, an Orange County developer, purchased the then seventy-one room property. In 1992 a Jack Nicklaus golf course was built, and subsequently a major renovation took place that completely re-configured the Palmilla into a 172-room/suite resort, including the Villa Cortez, a 10,000-s.f. villa, complete with its own private beach. It is said that if you have to ask the price of the villa, you can't afford to stay there. The opening of the newly renovated resort took place just shortly after John Travolta's colossal birthday bash at Palmilla in 2004. This was a favorite place of Clark Gable and today of Jennifer Anniston, John Mayer, Cameron Diaz and Drew Barrymore. I might add here that in 1990-1992, I worked with Don Koll on projects in the Northern California area. I found him to be extremely personable, and listening to his stories on Cabo, only deepened my wanting to be a part of what was happening there.

But as the Palmilla grew, Bud Parr became increasingly anxious to create his own private resort development. As a result, he sold his stake in the Palmilla and set off on a real estate search that ended with the purchase of a property at Rancho El Tule near Chileno Bay. To develop the property, he added partner Luis Coppola Bonillas in the ven-

Hotel Cabo San Lucas, 1962. Photo credit with permission: Cabo Living Magazine, Spring 2008 issue.

ture and began the quest to find enough fresh water for the hotel. Drill holes began to appear all around the property, and a rumor circulated that Parr had discovered a pirate map and was on the hunt for the buried treasure; after all, the place was named after the Chilean pirates who used to hide there and raid passing ships. In 1962, the Hotel Cabo San

Chileno Bay development with old Hotel Cabo San Lucas still intact, 2012. Photo credit with permission: Cabo Living Magazine, Winter 2014 issue.

Lucas opened with 125 rooms and suites that terraced down to the beach. The property featured very high-end appointments, service, and design, with multi-tier swimming pools, handmade furniture, and lush tropical landscaping. The chefs were Italian and Swiss, with Mexican bakers to assist. Parr himself brought a sculptor on site to carve over three-hundred pieces out of Cantera stone to decorate the resort. As did other luxury resorts, it became a haven for the Hollywood set: Lucille Ball, Barry Goldwater, John Wayne, Frank Sinatra, Kirk and Michael Douglas, Cary Grant, Raquel Welch, and more. With the hotel a success, Budd Parr sold a portion of his interest to Texas oilman David Halliburton Sr., who bought in as a partner, and as the opportunity arose, Parr continued to buy other land holdings to expand his base, including land at Cabo del Sol and Caleta Linda. The resort, however, was ultimately bought out in 2011 by a development group, Bald Mountain LLC, and the old hotel was demolished to make way for the new Chileno Bay Club, encompassing 1,260 acres, with two miles of coastline and a Tom Fazio eighteen-hole golf course. I recall on a visit prior to the demolition, enjoying the clubhouse view of the sea while sitting in an old chair possibly once shared by John Wayne or Frank Sinatra. They often visited to also enjoy the peace and serenity this view provided. A sense of nostalgia and sadness came across me knowing this would all be gone soon. In 2018, developer Discovery Land Group subsequently took over the development of the Chileno Bay resort.

Hacienda Cabo San Lucas, 1966. Source is three friends of Bette Sutherin. Photo credit: Richard Pearson.

As Parr was building the Hotel Cabo San Lucas, Rod Rodriquez was working on his own new venture, the first luxury hotel in Cabo San Lucas, the Hacienda Cabo San Lucas. It was located just behind what is now called Medano Beach and opened its doors in 1963. The hotel was designed in a colonial architectural style with balcony corridors and red tile roofs. The 1966 aerial picture really gives you a perspective on just how remote and isolated these one-off resorts were at the time. In 1970, the property was acquired by Western International Hotels of Mexico as Camino Real del Cabo San Lucas (now the Westin Hotel Group). In 1977, Budd Parr purchased the Camino Real del Cabo San Lucas and renamed it Hotel Hacienda Beach Resort. In 2005, the resort was sold to Don Koll and the old hotel was demolished. In partnership with Del Mar Development and Starwood Capital, Don Koll built and opened a new Hacienda in 2008 that encompassed 239 residences over 22 acres, with 109 beachfront villas.

Hacienda Cabo San Lucas, 1966. Photo originally published in the Baja Pony Express, 2011, sent in by Bill and Kay Barbour. Notice Hacienda in the center and cannery on far right.

Medano Beach, El Arco, and the area around Land's End are living symbols of Cabo San Lucas. Medano Beach stretches two miles from the mouth of the harbor along the coastline of the Bahia (Bay) San Lucas and is one of the only swimmable beaches in

Medano Beach. Photo credit: Dr. Mark Schrader, 2007, JPEG file

Medano Beach; Billygans, The Office and Mango Deck. Photo credit: Dr. Mark Schrader, 2007, JPEG file.

Cabo. From the late 1500s to the early 1800s, it was used as a pirate haven that gave cover to the buccaneers seeking to ambush gold-laden Spanish ships on their way back from the Philippines. Today the placid waters of the ocean have a welter of activity at the beach, complete with bikini's, boardshorts, drinks, people-watching, beach vendors, sunbathers, and music. Beach clubs vary in the "vibe" they provide. For example, Billygans, which is named after the TV show *Gilligan's Island* and used to have a similar wrecked boat, which was subsequently lost to the sea in Hurricane Odile, has drink, food, music, and sunbathing. Mango Deck, on the other hand is known for its raucous beach contests and sun-soaked debauchery. And last is the Office, which is an enjoyable umbrella-covered restaurant complete with tequila shots drawn from a holstered bandolier named "Rambo." Incredible views of the sea, the arch, and Land's End can be seen through the tabletops of ballasted buckets of beer, Michelada's (a beer-based Mexican cocktail), and tequila bottles. It is also the best debarkation point to Lovers Beach or Playa del Amor, known in older times as Playa Dona Chepa. Legend has it that a mysterious woman of the evening named Dona Chepa appropriated this beach for business purposes, hence the name Lovers Beach. Others say it is because it is where the Pacific melds with the Sea of Cortez. Once on Lovers Beach, you can walk across to the Pacific side, where the water is dangerous with rip tides, strong undercurrents, and turbulent seas hence perhaps its name, Divorce Beach. Not far from the beach are the underwater sand falls, a natural phenomenon discovered in the 1970s by Jacques-Yves Cousteau. True rivers of underwater sand here reach a depth of 98 ft. down to 394 ft. on a sloped descent of about 75 degrees. The great arch itself is the last point of uninterrupted land reaching down from Alaska to this final tip of the Baja at Land's End. It is the final gateway to the ocean that existed once, prior to the sea that surrounds it today. This is what postcards are made of and was a significant landmark to those who first came to the area.

With the new resorts opening, access to sportfishing in the waters off the Baja southern tip was becoming slightly more attainable for the few who could afford it. The area was nicknamed "Marlin Alley" and attracted big names to the area for the big game trophies of marlin, tuna, wahoo, and dorado. The photo shows two large gulf groupers or giant black sea bass from the old sportsman club in Loretto. In 1966, Richard Wilkes started two tag and release sport-fishing tournaments, the Classic and the Cortez Pacific, off the coast of Mexico to further enhance the sport and lure the tourists. He was friends with Bob Bisbee, who, later, in 1981, would bring a whole new meaning to sport fishing tournaments. In 1981, Bisbee held his first fishing tournament, with six boats and a $10,000 purse, and by 1983 it had grown to twenty-seven boats. It is now called the Bisbee's Black and Blue marlin tournament, held every October, and in 2006 the largest cash payout ever was made, at $4.165 million dollars.

Photo from an unknown source, found at the following site: bigfishesoftheworld.blogspot.com.

Bisbee fishing tournament start with the boats heading past Cabo Bello, 2019. Photo credit: Dr. Mark Schrader, 2019, JPEG file.

In 1972, Hotel Finisterra, was constructed, an engineering marvel with its cliff-side location on the Pacific side of Cabo San Lucas. Luis Coppola Bonillas, Luis Bulnes Molleda, and Paul Arechiga built this first hotel on the Pacific, and it is one of the original oceanfront hotels that is still standing today. It opened with fifty-six rooms and was the first hotel to stay open year-round. Luis Molleda sold his shares shortly after completion

The Finisterra, circa 1974. Photo from an unknown source, found on the following site: bdoutdoors.com.

in the late '70s to Luis Coppola to assist him in building his next project, the Solmar. In 1983, Keith Richards and Patti Hansen were wed there on December 18 in the Whale Watchers Bar. That event was seen by Sammy Hagar, and that led him to visit Cabo soon after for the very first time. The huge palapa restaurant that exists today by the pool can be easily seen from the air or sea and is a center piece of the resort. Another distinction of the property is that it is a nesting ground for the olive ridley sea turtles that arrive each year and subsequently call it home. The resort was redesigned and renamed Sandos Finisterra Los Cabos in 2014 and is now an all-inclusive resort.

Up until this point the Cabo area was the domain of the so-called beautiful people, well-heeled sport-fishing enthusiasts who arrived by their private yachts or by private plane landing on a dirt airstrip. This changed, however, in 1973 with the completion of the 1,000-mile Transpeninsular Highway that connects Cabo San Lucas to the U.S. border at Tijuana. This major project began almost two decades earlier, working south from Ensenada and outwards from the capital of La Paz. A dedication was held at the project's midpoint in Guerrero Negro in December of 1973. Now, for the first time, this narrow two-lane road could give access to the southern tip of the Baja for everyone and not just the wealthy. Mex 1, as it was

Transpeninsular Highway, circa 1974. Photo from an unknown source, found at the following site: bdoutdoors.com

called, brought along with it access to products and materials that would now enable the developmental visions of many to be realized in the Cabo San Lucas area. But at the same time, access to the Baja tip from both the water and the air was under way. In 1973, dredging of the Cabo San Lucas harbor also began. This would effectively re-shape the physical footprint of Cabo San Lucas, carving out a major marina that would assist in transforming

Cabo San Lucas Marina, 1980. Photo credit: Pedregal de Cabo San Lucas.

this area into a world-class destination. The photo of the marina is from 1980, just shortly after the dredging was completed. The original Hotel Hacienda can be seen on the left, sitting just up on Medano Beach, in the picture of the marina above. A year into the project, ferry services from Puerto Vallarta would begin, thus connecting the mainland of Mexico for the public by sea for the first time. (Ferry services ended in 1986) In 1975, the dredging was completed and space for the new three-hundred-slip full-service marina would now be ready for visiting yachts and sailboats.

Cabo-Puerto Vallarta ferry, circa 1980. Photo from an unknown source, found at the following site: facebook.com/groups/fotoantiquasbajacaliforniasur/.

Solmar Hotel, 2007. Most of the hotel was destroyed by Hurricane Odile in 2014 and rebuilt. Photo credit: Dr. Mark Schrader, JPEG file

Having sold his stake in the Finisterra, Luis Bulnes began his next venture with the building of the Solmar Hotel, a luxurious resort that opened in 1974. It was initially twenty rooms, nestled near the arch at Land's End, and, like the Finisterra, it too was located on the Pacific Ocean beach-side. It was nicknamed "the last resort" because of its southern most location and included a suite named the Ray Cannon Suite, which was literally built into the living rocks. After the completion of Hotel Solmar, Bulnes was looking for a new project. When a friend from Mexico City told him about a plan to film a movie in Cabo, Bulnes went to work to help make the motion picture *Fox Trot* with Peter O'Toole, Charlotte Rampling, Max von Sydow, and others in his hotel. In 1995, a major expansion took place by Bulnes changing the hotel into the Solmar Suites, followed by subsequent projects as part of what is now known as Grupo Solmar: Hotel Quinta del Sol, Playa Grande, and restaurants that include the El Galeon, La Fonda, Sea Queen, and Romeo y Julieta. It needs to be added here that Don Luis also built the largest sportfishing fleet in Cabo and has been one of, the people, if not the person, most responsible for the promotion and development of the sport in Cabo San Lucas. A statue of him stands today in front of the Marina Fundadores in Cabo San Lucas, honoring him for his contributions to Cabo. I stayed there during the construction of one of my homes and remember enjoying the sound of the waves.

As tourists flocked to the area and enjoyed the lifestyle, weather, and charm, many wanted to retire, live, or buy a second home or timeshare in Cabo. In 1974, architect Manuel Diaz Rivera purchased approximately 250 acres that would become the community of Pedregal de Cabo San Lucas. In 1975, he laid the first stone of its many cobbled streets. It was the first gated residential community in the Cabo area, and with its views up the mountain, it gained a reputation for housing the elite and celebrities. It has been rumored, rightly or not, that Sylvester Stallone, Eddie Murphy, George Clooney, and others have or had homes here. Today, it has 950 lots with an average size of 7,000 s.f. and encompasses 360 acres.

The Pedregal, circa 2014. Photo from an unknown source, found at the following site: cbriveras.com

Starting at the same time as the Pedregal, Guillermo Salas Peyro purchased property about five kilometers out of town from Cabo to also become one of the original master-planned residential communities. Cabo Bello consists of 359 homes, lots, and condominiums with access to the Sea of Cortez. The very first fideicomiso was issued on a property from here (the legal mechanism whereby foreigners can own property that is in the country's coastal or border areas). I personally had a home here for many years, and since my ownership, it has become a gated community similar to the Pedregal and others.

Cabo Bello, 2007. Photo credit: Dr. Mark Schrader, 2007, JPEG file.

Not much existed in the way of accommodations/tourism in the early days of the Southern Baja peninsula aside from these few luxury hotels with their private airstrips. For those who may have traveled here in recent years, it has to be tough to imagine how it was then. However, in 1976, the Mexican government decided to have its national trust for the promotion of tourism, FONATUR, begin making Cabo one of its top three beach resort projects. A twenty-year development plan was drawn up, which included building a highway linking the towns of San Jose and Cabo San Lucas, developing the airport in San Jose, and expanding the marina in Cabo. Up until then, the airport in Cabo had existed just behind the Hotel Hacienda and would interfere with the marina expansion project, so it was moved, and the first bulldozer and grader used are now displayed on elevated pedestals located in the Plaza Pioneros parking lot. In 1977, the San Jose airport opened a major expansion that had the capacity to accommodate thousands of passengers per day, giving international access to the coastline. The modern era of development was about to hit Cabo in a big way. In the picture, the old airport behind the Hotel Hacienda can be seen circa 1960 and where it would be in 2012. In 1986 and again in 1997, the Los Cabos International Airport was expanded, further accommodating the swell in those wanting to enjoy the area. The first airline to service Baja Sur was Aeronaves de Mexico, which in

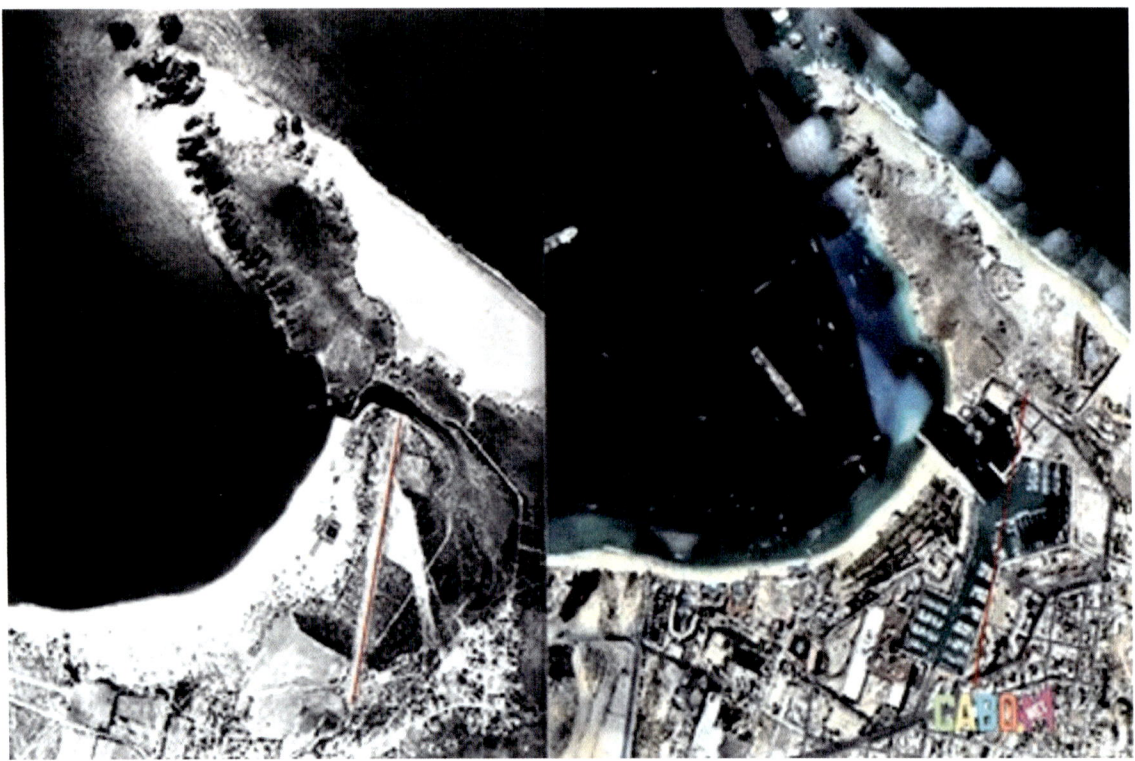

Old Cabo San Lucas Airport location circa 1960 and 1997. Photo from an unknown source, found at the following site: aviada.blogspot.com

1941 began flights between the mainland and La Paz. After World War II, early airlines and air taxi services included independent bush pilots and companies such as Servicios Aereos de La Paz (later Aerocalifornia) and Lineas Aereas del Pacifico. But it was only after 1962, when Aeronaves de Mexico began scheduled air traffic, that the airline industry started to make an impact in bringing tourists to Baja California Sur. In that year, DC-6 propeller service began between Los Angeles and La Paz, followed by the first DC-8 jets in 1966.

Having the foresight to see the development potential in Cabo, David Halliburton Sr. had bought into the Hotel Cabo San Lucas, as noted earlier, and spent a lot of time there with his wife and children. He was told by his father, Erle, that he looked like a twin dolphin when he played in and out of the waters around Cabo, and the name stuck, leading

Twin Dolphin Hotel, 1993. Photo taken from an unknown source, but can be found at the following site: cabosfinestrealestate.com.

him to name his own forty-seven-foot cruiser the same. But while staying at the Hotel Cabo San Lucas, he was very vocal about improvements he thought should be made and repeatedly mentioned these to Matt Parr, who finally told him, "If you don't like it here, go build your own hotel." And so he did, and in 1972 he began work on a hotel to be aptly named the Twin Dolphin. The location selected was near Bahia Santa Maria, along what is now referred to as the tourist corridor, and it opened in 1977. The hotel had thirteen cabanas, which, in total, housed forty-six deluxe rooms and six suites, complete with first-class cotton linens, and imported soaps, and lotions, complemented by upscale dining, which helped to make this a haven of sophistication. With the opening of the highway and the airport, his timing could not have been better to provide such a refuge, complete with a dramatic swimming pool that overlooked the Sea of Cortez. The hotel was closed in 2006 and was subsequently demolished, and it has since become the site for the new Montage Los Cabos Resort and adjacent Maravilla Los Cabos residential community developments.

With the airport now expanded, the highway open, and a fully equipped and modern marina available, Cabo began to explode with growth as developers hoping to capitalize came from all over. Remember, up until now, only a handful of resorts were available and catered only to the pampered crowd who could afford their luxurious accommodations and prices. Roads were still dirt, Highway 91 from Todos Santos to Cabo had just been paved in 1985, large tracts of open land existed, and little to no infrastructure had been built- no water system, no sewage systems, minimal electricity to speak of, etc. But with FONATUR coming in and the demand for access enabled, this once sleepy fishing village was about to change in a major way. The term "Los Cabos" was now used to describe the area of Cabo San Lucas and San Jose del Cabo. It means "capes" and, from a marketing standpoint, was brilliant. The unique combination of desert and sea had people saying, "Los Cabos is like a Palm Springs with an ocean." One development after the other launched in the Los Cabos area. In an attempt to capture this explosion, a number of these notable ventures, including some of the clubs and restaurants, follow:

At a time in the 1980s when the political and economic climate in Mexico was precarious at best, Don Koll continued to invest in the Los Cabos area. In 1985, Koll offered that Robert Day join him in a partnership to buy from Budd Parr the 1,800-acre Cabo del Sol property, which had 20 miles of oceanfront. After the purchase, they sold off two small parcels that later became the sites for the Sheraton and the Fiesta Americana hotels. The project initially was envisioned to consist of three hotels with 2,000 rooms, 3,400 condominiums and homes, three golf courses, a health spa, tennis courts, and a shopping village. This was the largest undertaking of its kind ever in the area and unique for the number of home lots for sale. In 1994, the second Jack Nicklaus signature golf course in Mexico was opened on the property, and within the first year of operation, the Cabo del Sol Golf Course was ranked number 68 in the world by *Golf Digest* magazine. This put Los Cabos

Cabo del Sol, 2019. Photo credit with permission: Cabo Living Magazine, Winter, 2019 issue.

on the map as a premier golf destination and was the forerunner of the collection of leading courses that exist in Cabo today. Robert Day eventually bought out Don Koll and became the sole owner and operator of the development.

Mike Grzanich came to Cabo in 1959 on a tuna boat. He has seen a lot over the years but also has a lot in his Latitude 22+ Roadhouse Restaurant and Bar in Cabo San Lucas. The restaurant is packed with fishing and marine memorabilia, life preservers from notable ships, tons of old photos, over five-hundred some odd license plates, business cards everywhere, and more. One of the more notable paraphernalia is "Jake," a 1,078-pound blue marlin caught in December of 1992, which hangs in the bar. It is also known for the "No Bad Days" decal that originated from here. The restaurant started back around 1988 in Cabo but moved out to its current location not far from Costco in March of 2004. It has ocean views of the Bahia San Lucas and is casual, not pretentious, just affordable good food and drink. This is a colorful local hangout that you will not find elsewhere in Los Cabos, but one that adds to the overall ambiance and character of Cabo.

Latitude 22+/Roadhouse Restaurant and Bar. Photo is from an unknown source, found at the following site: vacations-to-cabo-san-lucas.com

On the complete other side of the spectrum from the Roadhouse is the Hotel ME Cabo. In the early seventies, Guillermo Salas Peyro bought 7.5 acres of land near Medano Beach which he subsequently put into the development company he co-founded with Eduardo Sanchez Navarro. In 1988, the Melia San Lucas would open on this

Melia Cabo San Lucas now called ME, circa 1992. Photo from an unknown source, found at the following site: yahglobal.com.

property, which is now known as ME Cabo. The ME has 162 rooms, a beachside pool, three restaurants, four bars, and a full-service spa. It is close to downtown, the mall, and Cabo San Lucas marina, making it an ideal location for all activities. This is now a trendy social hub of activity with a mix of local and international jetsetters. Bali beds, VIP bottle service, and an on-site DJ round out the pool scene. The ME was renovated in late 2015 following Hurricane Odile and is owned by the biggest developer in Cabo, the Questro Group. You can see in the photo that in the background, the Casa Dorado and the new Hacienda do not exist yet. As a side note, Guillermo Salas was also responsible for the opening and startup of the first radio station in Cabo San Lucas in 1988. Called "Cabo Mil," it is still operating today on 96.3 FM.

A fisherman by the name of Oscar Montano Herrera, nicknamed Don Yoka, used to own a small home by Medano Beach in the 1960s and was considered by many at that time to be a pioneer of the fishing trade in the Cabo area. In the mid 1980s, a developer by the name of Juan Esquivel purchased the property from Herrera and built one of the first hotels on Medano Beach, named the Bahia Hotel. Juan was also the owner of the Gaviotas ("seagulls" in English) fishing fleet and an avid supporter of sport-fishing in Cabo. In 2007, a development group from New York subsequently purchased the property and had plans to re-purpose it. However, as a result of the recession that followed, they

Bahia Hotel, circa 2019. Photo credit with permission: Bahia Hotel and Beach House

changed their initial plans and instead only repositioned the existing hotel, including the addition of a quality high-end restaurant/bar. In 2010, the newly renovated eighty-eight room hotel opened keeping the same name, but with "Bar Esquina" adding a new stylish touch. This is all about location, location, location. It is in the heart of the Medano Beach district, just two blocks from the beach, with easy access to a clutch of great bars and

Sur Beach House, 2019. Photo credit with permission: Hotel Bahia

restaurants. In 2016, another opportunity arose for the Bahia, and they purchased the Las Palmas Lobster House, which was right on Medano Beach. This would give their guests an opportunity to have direct access to the beach, and from that, Sur Beach House was born. This is an upscale club complete with an exceptional chef-inspired restaurant where you can dine on the beachside open-air porch, inside, or right on the beach itself. Rosè all day, Champagne, or hand-crafted cocktails flow freely here, prepared by a personal mixologist or selected by the in-house sommelier. On the beach are chaise lounge chairs, side tables, and personalized waiter service for food or drink. This is one of the few places where you can get decent wine by the bottle (served in actual wine coolers with ice) on the beach.

Cruise ships in Bahia Cabo, 2009. Photo credit: Dr. Mark Schrader, JPEG file.

Photo credit: Dr. Mark Schrader, Tesoro, 2007, JPEG file.

The dredging of the marina created some of the most valuable land to be developed in downtown Cabo San Lucas as well as laid the foundation for the city to accommodate cruise ships. This is an important source of revenue, and in September of 2009, five-cruise ships laid anchor in the Bahia of Cabo San Lucas, the first time ever for that many. Small businesses started to pop up all around the new marina, catering especially to the fishing trade, tourists eager to take a chance at deep-sea fishing, and now the cruise ship passengers. A mammoth waterfront development, however, was also in the works at the north end of the marina that would literally span the entire border, called Plaza Las Glorias. It was a mixed-use development, one of the first in Cabo, that would have retail, timeshares, and a hotel. By 1990, construction was completed on the five-story 286-room Plaza Las Glorias Hotel, and it was opened to the public. In the same year, it also served as the headquarters for the Bisbee fishing tournament, and today it stands as an ideal location for any traveling angler to stay and make that six-a.m. charter. In 2004, Steadfast Properties purchased the hotel and renamed it Costa Real Cabo Resort. In turn, they sold it to Tesoro, who, in January of 2011, sold it to Wyndham Hotel and Resorts, LLC.

In 1990, the population of Baja California Sur was now over 637,000, and the number of travelers visiting the Los Cabos area exceeded 260,000. This remarkable growth led to many entrepreneurial ventures to fulfil the needs of the area, not the least of which was undertaken by a young musician by the name of Sammy Hagar, who was in Van Halen. As noted prior, he visited Cabo for the first time shortly after seeing Keith Richards getting married there in 1983 and booked a full week at the Twin Dolphin in October to celebrate his birthday. The following year, he bought a home in the Terrasol area and would invite his brother and sister to join him annually in October to celebrate their birthdays, which were in the same week as his. The love of the area led him to open a nightclub called the Cabo Wabo, named after the band's hit single by the same name, in 1990. At first, it was going to be located in the old cannery, and the slogan to be used was "Where the land ends, the party begins," but after looking at all the options, he chose a site in town off Vicente Guerrero street. It was at first an unknown spot where he and other musicians in town would meet up, have a few cocktails and play. But as time went on, word got out about the new nightclub, and by 1994, the famous "Birthday Bash" would be sold out henceforth. You never knew when he would show up and play, nor who would join him,

Cabo Wabo, start of construction. Opened 1990. Photo credit with permission: Cabo Wabo Cantina.

it was all part of the mystique and intrigue of going to Cabo Wabo. I personally have enjoyed some of those random visits, with names like Toby Keith, Michael Bolton, Michael Anthony, and Kenny Chesney joining Sammy on stage. I also recall back in my early days in Cabo that the streets surrounding Cabo Wabo were dirt turning quickly to a sloppy mess after rain, making getting back to my hotel difficult after a few… libations there. New Year's at the Cabo Wabo with Sammy jamming was a family tradition of ours for many years, and this is one of my favorite shots of Sammy from one of those nights. In 2006, the Cabo Wabo tequila brand was launched, and subsequently, Sammy sold his interest in it in 2010 to the Campari group.

Sammy Hagar, 2009. Photo credit: Dr. Mark Schrader, 2009, JPEG file.

The Office, 2006. Photo credit: Dr. Mark Schrader, 2006, JPEG file.

With all the new tourists coming in to town, many were looking for quality places to enjoy the cuisine of Baja. Edith Jimenez started her entrepreneurial career by opening a clothing store in Cabo San Lucas. But when a small beach-side restaurant on Medano Beach became available in 1988, she changed vocation and opened her own eatery. The place was called Sinolosense, but no sign to that effect existed. Only a sign on the establishment next to it that read "The Office" was visible. So, when describing where her place was located, people would say it was next to the sign "The Office," and hence the name today. It became one of only a handful of places where you could eat or drink at the beach. Concern, however, over threats by the landowners to throw her off the beach had Edith looking for a new location. She decided on a spot just off the beach where she had formerly worked, called Estella's by the Sea. She expressed her interest in the location and in 1994 when it became available, she took over the restaurant, calling it Edith's. The pictures I took show the front of the Office from the beach and of Edith's, highlighting their famous Mexican coffee being made.

Edith's, 2006. Photo credit: Dr. Mark Schrader, Edith's, 2006, JPEG file.

Dating back to at least 1989 is another nightclub that initially opened as a fresh seafood restaurant but, over time, transformed into one of the iconic late-night hot spots in

El Squid Roe, 1989. Photo from an unknown source, found at the following site: lapazantiqua-sudcalifornia.blogspot.com.

El Squid Roe, 2019. Photo from an unknown source, found at the following site: garzablancaresort.com

downtown Cabo: El Squid Roe. It is now a three-story night club, dance hall, and restaurant all in one. It is a high energy, boisterous environment for those wanting to kick up their heels. El Squid Roe is frequently visited by Enrique Iglesias, Michael Jordan, Snoop Dogg, Rihanna, Beyoncè and more. One visitor said, "Your dancing shoes are gonna end up with some thin soles." From the picture, you can see just how barren things were in 1989, along the unpaved main street of Lazaro Cardenas.

Giggling Marlin. Photo credit with permission: Giggling Marlin

The oldest bar in Cabo is said to be the Giggling Marlin dating back to 1984, and it was once the only bar in downtown. It is on the main street into town on Marina Boulevard. It is purportedly home of the Hop, Skip and Go Naked drink and is known for hanging people upside down on a fish scale for a photograph. Food, drink, and floor shows involving contestants from the bar make this a spirited place. It has recently produced its own brand of blue weber agave tequila, which is now available, using only the hand-selected hearts of the plant, giving it a smooth, elegant taste. Its famous motto is "If our food, drink, and services aren't up to your standards, please lower your standards."

Giggling Marlin, 2008. Photo credit: Craig Schrader, 2008, JPEG file.

Westin Hotel and Resort, 2018. Photo from an unknown source, found at the following site: hotel-scoop.com

With the hardships of the 1980s over, a new resurgence in tourism began in Baja Sur, as exemplified by the bold design statement at the Westin Hotel and Resort. The resort flows in color and shape with the desert land that surrounds it and also complements the ocean it stands before. It was built in 1991 and opened in 1992, initially as the Hotel Conrad, on the corridor just southwest of Punta Bella. This is the first hotel with such height and grandeur. The main building was designed by Javier Sordo Madaleno and initially had 243 guestrooms, but as part of its renovations following Hurricane Odile in 2017, it changed to 147 suites, now called "villas". The complex has three to nine story towers (two of which interconnect), a gym, a 10,000-s.f. "Otomispa," three pools, and multiple restaurants. A unique characteristic is that every room has an excellent ocean view, as the towers were designed in such a way that all windows are situated on the convex side, facing the sea. Its presidential suite is a favorite among celebrities such as Michael Jordan and Adam Sandler.

I recall standing on Medano Beach, looking at the construction of the Pueblo Bonito Blanco, and wondering who would buy into that timeshare development, as it was so far out of town. I could not have been more wrong. In 1990, Don Bisbee sold his Medano Beach property to the Pueblo Bonito Resorts, co-owned by Ernesto Coppel and Mark Kronemeyer, which developed on Medano Beach both the Bonito Blanco and then the Bonito Rose. The term "Blanco" was added later to distinguish the resort and for its pure white exterior. The hotel has blue domes that architecturally were designed to blend with the sea it faces, and it has a Mediterranean-style ambiance throughout. In 1991, Pueblo Bonito Banco opened with 148 ocean-view suites, each with its own kitchenette. This is

Bonito Rose on right, Bonito Blanco center and Melia Cabo San Lucas on left, 2007. Photo credit: Dr. Mark Schrader, 2007, JPEG file.

an all-inclusive property. In 1997, the Pueblo Bonito Rose, named for its soft red facade, opened with 260 ocean-view suites and an onsite spa. The exterior décor and that of its public spaces is modeled on ancient Rome. The lobby sets the tone, with Romanesque busts, rich tapestries, and a rotunda topped by a central oculus. This is also an all-inclusive hotel with kitchenettes in all the rooms.

In Cabo, large holdings of land were diminishing now, and attention turned back to the corridor, the area between Cabo San Lucas and San Jose, where the original Hotel Cabo San Lucas, Palmilla, and Twin Dolphin were built. It was no longer pioneers of Cabo or individuals building these resorts but large corporate conglomerates that had entered the Cabo hospitality market. In 1992, one of the first of these large hotel groups, the Hilton Group, announced its new hotel, which was to be built on 11.3 acres of beachfront property with hacienda-style accommodations just southwest of Playa Cabo Real. And just to the west of it, the Questro Group built another hotel, named the Melia Real Cabo San Lucas, which is easily identifiable by its large glass pyramid roof structure near the entry. It now has 350 rooms and has been renamed, as part of a new branding effort by Questro, as Paradisus Los Cabos. Both of these hotels were severely hit by Hurricane Odile and went through major renovations in 2015/2016.

Cabo Surf Hotel. Photo credit with permission: Cabo Surf Hotel and Spa.

Originally a beach house just south of Mirador Costa Azul, between Punta Palmilla and the beaches leading to San Jose, is the Cabo Surf Hotel, which is part of the Balderrama Hotel Collection. The family purchased the property in 1994 and has since turned it into a small thirty-seven-room hotel and spa. Not to be missed here is the 7 Seas seafood grille, which specializes in fresh sea food from the local Baja waters. The surf break out in front is also renowned, and from the 7 Seas terrace you can watch the surfers, a favorite pastime of mine during lunch there. Legendary surfer Mike Doyle used to enjoy the surfing there in the early 1990s, and the surf school that exists on the property is still to this day named after him, even though he has since passed on. The beach itself is also known locally as Old Man and Playa Acapulquito. Complete with the Sea Spa, this small boutique hotel is reminiscent of a California-style beach house.

Mike Doyle Surf School. Photo credit with permission: Cabo Surf Hotel and Spa.

Hacienda del Mar. Photo with permission: Grupo Olarena.

The two-spin off parcels from Don Koll and Robert Days purchase of Cabo del Sol in 1985 went toward the development of the Sheraton and Fiesta Americana hotels. The Sheraton is part of the Hacienda del Mar development, which is owned by Grupo Olarena, and began construction in 1994 when renowned architects Wimberly Allison Tong and Goo laid out the design concept for the twenty-acre-acre resort. The Sheraton itself has 270 suites, all decorated in a combination of traditional Mexican colonial elements and stylish Mediterranean finishes. In addition, it has eight restaurants, four snack bars, five swimming pools, a private beach, a snorkeling pool, a gym and the Cactus spa. On the property is a favorite oceanside restaurant of mine named Pitahayas, complete with an enormous palapa over the main dining area. It opened May 21, 1995, with Pan-Asian cuisine but has since changed to a combination of Asian and traditional Mexican fare after an extensive remodel in 2015. A four-hundred-bottle wine cellar named La Cava de Santiago exists under the restaurant. The Fiesta Americana was opened in 1999 and is owned by Grupo Posadas, Mexico's largest hotel operator. It has 248 rooms,

Pitahayas Restaurant. Photo credit with permission: Grupo Olarena.

seven restaurants, five bars, and five swimming pools. It was one of the first resorts to open after months of repairing the damage left by Hurricane Odile, as the resort officially re-opened to guests in November 2014 with new paint, new furniture, and a new lobby, a spa, restaurants, and landscaping. On October 26, 2002, President George Bush and his wife attended a dinner there for APEC forum participants hosted by Presidente Vicente Fox.

In the late 1990s and early 2000s getting simple tasks accomplished by U.S. standards was still pretty cumbersome. For example, to get a simple key made, you had to go to a special business that specialized in making keys. Groceries were obtained from small grocery stores/markets, paying bills had to be done in person, and hardware items were purchased through small businesses such as El Arco or Dos Hermanos. But with the rapid growth came more investment, and with it emerged large retail outlets. In October of 2003, Costco opened its doors to a crowd of amazed ex-pats and locals; in October 2004, Home Depot opened across from the Cabo Bello Community; and shortly thereafter, Walmart opened in the new Plaza San Lucas. The conveniences of "home" had come to Cabo. There is no doubt that this hurt many of the small business entities in Cabo, and at the same time, it left many of the ex-pats living there feeling like it was time to move on and seek quieter surroundings, perhaps on the East Cape or San Jose. They coined the phrase "BC," Before Costco, to describe the way things "used" to be. Cabo had gotten too big for them. The sleepy little fishing village had grown up.

Querencia Clubhouse, circa 2019. Photo from an unknown source, found at the following site: jetsetmag.com.

In the year 2000, Baja Sur was nearing half a million in population, and the prosperity of the economy was showing up everywhere. Workers were coming to Cabo from all over Mexico because of the abundance of jobs, the high quality of life, and the higher pay.

Capitalizing on this, Querencia came onto the San Jose del Cabo scene in 2000. Set across from the Cabo Surf Hotel, it is a large 1,800-acre master-planned development with a 320-acre Tom Fazio golf course. The development has changed hands several times but is now held by Cornerstone Holdings LLC. It is a gated community that sits at the high point near San Jose and Highway 1, with custom residences from $750,000 to 12 million dollars.

In 2002, the Auberge Group decided to enter the Cabo San Lucas market by opening Esperanza (meaning "hope"). Located in Punta Ballena, it brought a new wave of luxury design and style to the coastline. Designed by Backen/Gillan architects in association with Mario Maldonado of GV Arquitectos, the resort opened with fifty-seven-rooms. In 2009, it was renovated, and eight new suites (two on the beach) were added along with a spacious penthouse, a palapa-style yoga studio, and a swim-up infinity bar/pool, all adding to the comfort and relaxation of the resort. It originally was a Relais & Chateaux collection hotel as part of the Auberge Group. Known as one of the most private and intimate resorts

Esperanza Resort. Photo credit with permission: Auberge Resorts Collection.

around, Esperanza hosted numerous world leaders and celebrities, including former President Barack Obama and the U.S. delegation during the G20 Mexico Summit in 2012. In similar fashion, it is home away from home for celebrities such as Gwyneth Paltrow, Fergie, Chris Martin, Josh Duhamel, and Leonardo DiCaprio.

The Questro Group, having great success with their newly opened properties in the Cabo San Lucas area, took on another project on Medano Beach just west of their Melia Cabo San Lucas (ME) development: Casa Dorada Los Cabos Resort and Spa. In 2005, the seven-story high-end resort on five acres began construction. It was the first to offer a members-only private vacation club resort environment with 154 residences. In 2008, the doors opened, literally onto the beach, and attracted those wanting a relaxed tropical style of ownership. The resort has its share of celebrities too, with Paris Hilton, David DeLuise, Chelsea Kane, and Tommy Lee being among those seen there.

Casa Dorada under construction, 2007, with the Melia Cabo San Lucas to the right of it and Pueblo Bonito Blanco next to it. Photo credit: Dr. Mark Schrader, 2007, JPEG file.

Not to be outdone, in 2002, Ken Jowdy, CEO and founder of Diamante Cabo San Lucas and Legacy Properties LLC, began planning an ambitious development called Diamante on the Pacific side of Cabo. It is a luxury master-planned resort community situated on approximately 1,500 acres of Pacific coastline that opened in late 2009. The grand opening included the premiere of the Dunes Course, a private course designed by Davis Love III and ranked thirty-eighth in the world on *GOLF Magazine's* top one-hundred list. In December 2014, Oasis, the first par 3 short course ever designed by Tiger Woods, opened here also.

Diamante Cabo San Lucas. Photo credit: Google Earth

The United States recession of 2007-2009 created a lull in the development of Los Cabos. The market was severely affected, and most projects were abandoned or halted altogether. In the following years, the recovery was gradual, and just when the market was once again steady, Hurricane Odile hit Cabo in 2014, causing severe damage to an extensive amount of properties throughout Baja Sur. Odile is tied for the most intense landfall tropical cyclone to hit the Baja Sur area, with the other being Hurricane Olivia in 1967. The devastation was widespread, but being "Cabo Strong" or the other term used locally, "Unstoppable," the area rebounded and development moved forward in a new and dramatic way. Seemingly unfazed, the corridor between Cabo and

Hurricane Odile damage with Pueblo Bonito Blanco in background, Medano Beach 2014. Photo from an unknown source, found at the following site: lapazantiqua-sudcalifornia.blogspot.com.

Hurricane Odile damage, beach in front of Hacienda del Mar, 2014. Photo from an unknown source, found at the following site: first2board.com.

San Jose erupted into a building frenzy with massive hotel projects that tout pillow-topped beds, infinity-edged pools, wine bars, and fairway-fronting brilliance. At the same time, numerous hotels that had been damaged by the hurricane took advantage of the down-time and chose to refresh and/or expand their properties, providing new places to wine, dine, and enjoy the sun. Highway 1 was lined with cars and buses belonging to hundreds of workers working on the collection of new hotels going up along the corridor. It was an unprecedented time of growth.

In 2018, over 2.6 million tourists visited Los Cabos, as it has become the go-to luxury destination for those looking to enjoy the azure waters of the Sea of Cortez, golf with killer ocean views, or just be spoiled poolside with an umbrella-garnished cocktail in hand, followed by a rejuvenating massage. Already with more five-star hotels than anywhere else in Latin America, the corridor saw the opening of even more hotels in 2018, illustrating the dramatic growth and the shift to extravagant resorts that are massive in size and complexity. For example, the Le Blanc Spa and Resort, owned by Palace Resorts, which has 373 rooms, is a smoke-free environment, and has an adult-only concept and a 29,000-s,f. spa, opened on the corridor in 2018. The Viceroy, located just as you enter San Jose del Cabo from the east, with 192 rooms and elevated walkways under which water flows directly from the Sea of Cortez, designed by architect Miguel Angel Aragone and owned by the Viceroy Hotel Group, also opened in 2018. The Cabo Azul Resort and Spa, with interior design by Dodd Mitchell, 326 suites and villas, the PAZ spa, a tri-level infinity pool, and multiple restaurants/cafes, owned by Diamond Resorts International out of Las Vegas, opened on twelve ocean-front acres on the corridor in 2018.

Solaz Signature Suites. Photo credit with permission: Grupo Olarena.

The Solaz Signature Suites, part of Marriott's Luxury Collection, opened on the corridor just south of Tequila Cove Beach in 2018, as well. The Solaz, which is on thirty-four acres and was designed by Sordo Madaleno, exemplifies the "new" luxury in Cabo. It is a stunning property, six stories in height, with a massive museum-like entrance, 127 rooms (115 are deluxe and 12 presidential), three restaurants, five swimming pools (two of which are Olympic size), and a wine cave with over 2,500 vintages. Guests there are welcomed by their own designated "artisan" butlers who assist them to their rooms and curate any personalized excursions they may wish during their stay. Ojo de Liebre, the 10,000-s.f. spa, offers Ayurvedic treatments, referring to the science of life and pressure points (I did not know, either). Times have changed, indeed. La Deriva is one of the newest restaurants to hit the Los Cabos scene, and with its Northern Italian cuisine using Baja fresh products, it is a wonderful addition to the Solaz. Set just back from the ocean waters and sandy beach, the location is ideal for any occasion.

Montage Los Cabos, 2018. Photo credit with permission: Montage Los Cabos

The Montage Los Cabos Resort and adjacent Maravilla Los Cabos residential community are built on the old Twin Dolphin Hotel site at Santa Maria Bay, as mentioned earlier. The resort, which opened in May of 2018, is situated on thirty-nine acres and has 122 rooms with ocean views, outside showers, and terraces. In addition, there are three casas, two presidential suites, and fifty-two full-ownership residences. The presidential suites are 2,695 s.f., each with two-bedrooms and come with a large pool located directly on the beach. The casas are private compounds that each contain 10,865 s.f. of living area, ranging from three to five bedrooms, and come with private chefs, personalized spa treatments, large private terraces with outdoor cooking facilities, a private infinity pool and Jacuzzi, a private beach bed, and even your own mezcal tasting. The spa is the largest in Los Cabos to date, at over 40,000 s.f. Here you can try the "jewel of the Baja" therapy, which involves the use of the Damiana plant, herbs, and agave honey all in a wrap. The golf club that is available still uses the Twin Dolphin name and is a Fred Couples-designed course that has views of the Sea of Cortez from every hole.

Back in Cabo now, things are also booming again, with luxurious resorts being developed and constructed. The Cape, a Thompson Hotel, which is now part of the world of Hyatt, opened in 2015, located near the southernmost tip of Monuments Beach. It is a 165-room resort with two restaurants, two pools (one with a swim-up bar and the other built into the natural rock), a roof top open-air lounge restaurant and bar, and a fitness center and spa. Each room has outdoor terraces to view the arch (El Arco) and the Bahai (bay) of Cabo San Lucas.

The Cape, a Thompson Hotel. Photo credit with permission: The Cape, a Thompson Hotel.

Cabo has come a long way from the 1950s to now. Over the past fifty plus years, the cacti and dirt have turned into grand extravagant resorts that make this part of the Baja a modern world-class destination. Upscale resorts with broad appeal now dot the landscape of this once quiet Mexican destination and have turned it into more of an international resort getaway. Between 2017 and 2021, more than 4,700 hotel rooms will be built in the Los Cabos area. If you add that to the existing 16,474 rooms, it will represent an increase of over 28.5%. The growth in rooms will, however, allow the destination to remain a favorite of the international jet set and have enough rooms to handle the expected influx of tourists. In just two years, the number of tourists arriving by air has increased by 11.6%. Over the thirty-eight years I have been coming to Cabo, it has been amazing to see the "Old Baja" transform into the now contemporary architecture that is modifying the traditional landscape of Los Cabos and allowing the destination to compete with other international resorts. What's next for Cabo remains to be seen, but no doubt it will remain an iconic destination for years to come.

Cabo Halloween Bash Triathlon, 1988. Chris Ogg on the left, myself in the center and Bob Jackson on the right; my fellow participants. I remember floating in the Melia Cabo San Lucas pool, which had just opened up, the morning after the race with my eyes half shut and seeing Chris at the opposite end with his head half submerged feeling my pain also. Cabo baby!

About the author: Dr. Mark Schrader lives in Scottsdale, Arizona with a second home in Cabo San Lucas. He has a masters of architecture and doctorate in business administration. He has also written the book, *"A True African Safari." "The Wildlife, Culture, People and Politics of Zimbabwe, July 2008"*. He is married to his lovely bride Kim. To-gether, they have three sons and two daughters.

Appendix

Please note that I have attempted to verify and identify the copyright holder of each image used. In many instances, though, I could not identify the copyright owner. If you are the copyright holder of any image used and I have not already obtained your permission, please contact me so I can give you the proper credit.

Whale tails, 2015 Photo credit: Dr. Mark Schrader, JPEG file.

Beach vendors on Medano Beach, 2019. Photo credit: Kimberly Schrader, JPEG file.

Deep sea fishing: the early morning start, Cabo, 2015. Photo credit: Dr. Mark Schrader, JPEG file.

Made in the USA
Las Vegas, NV
18 December 2021